# Bearers of an Idle Tale

# Bearers of an Idle Tale

## *Women's Authority in a Credibility Economy*

2024 Madeleva Lecture in Spirituality

**Natalia Imperatori-Lee**

Paulist Press
New York / Mahwah, NJ

Book and cover design by Lynn Else



Library of Congress Control Number: 2024952126

ISBN 978-0-8091-5750-1 (paperback)
ISBN 978-0-8091-8917-5 (ebook)

Published by Paulist Press
997 Macarthur Boulevard
Mahwah, NJ 07430
www.paulistpress.com

Printed and bound in the
United States of America

# Contents

Preface . . . . . . . . . . . . . . . . . . . . . . . . . . . . vii

Introduction . . . . . . . . . . . . . . . . . . . . . . . . . . 1

I. Experiential Foundations . . . . . . . . . . . . . . . . . . . 3

II. Women's Experience in the Shadow of Epistemic Injustice . . . . . . . . . . . . . . . . . . . . . . . 9

III. The Church and the Credibility Economy. . . . . . 17

IV. Conclusions . . . . . . . . . . . . . . . . . . . . . . . . 23

Notes . . . . . . . . . . . . . . . . . . . . . . . . . . . . . 29

# Preface

OVER THE YEARS, I've realized that I am enthralled by stories. Whether the family gossip I overheard in my youth, or the books that I consume in rapid succession during stressful seasons of life (I think I read ten books in the week after my father's sudden death in 1994), stories have intrigued and sustained me. Unsurprisingly, the story of the incarnation and the resurrection, and the story of the communal response to these realities that we know now to be the church, has proven to be the most fascinating tale of all, at least to this ecclesiologist.

Stories tell us who we are, invite us to deeper self-understanding and coax us to empathy, to solidarity, and to action. Stories can reveal reality to us, or they can be used to conceal ugly, uncomfortable truths. Because of this, many stories, a mosaic of stories, can prove more reliable than a single narrative in portraying the fullness and complexity of reality. In short, stories matter. But hearing stories is not enough.

In my first book, *Cuéntame*, I wrote extensively about the importance of narratives—demographic, historical, and aesthetic—in the work of ecclesiology. I stressed how impoverished Catholic ecclesiology was by the deductive approach that characterized its dominant methodology. Many ecclesiologies begin with doctrines, like the four marks of the church, and then proceed to deduce how these marks are present in the ecclesial community. Instead, I proposed an inductive methodology that began with the narratives that revealed the reality of the People of God.

*Cuéntame* intentionally broadens the scope of narratives that "count" for understanding the nature and mission of the church. These include broad demographic studies that reveal who makes up the church and how they worship, expansive historical narratives that open up our idea of what "American" Catholicism has meant and might mean in the future, and artistic "texts" like short stories, novels, and even artwork by Latinas and Chicanas. My aim in the book was to capture as many stories as I could and present them as integral to the story of U.S. Catholicism. If people hear these, I believed, then we can reorient our understanding of church, make it truer, because it will be more grounded in reality.

The injunction in *Cuéntame* was to listen, to open our ears and hearts and minds to a story of U.S. Catholicism that included the Latinx experience as an integral, driving force, present in this country from a time before even the thirteen colonies. With time, however, I realized that mere listening can promote the illusion of inclusion, or to put it less maliciously, listening is not a surefire path to conversion of mind or heart. Like the concepts of "tolerance" or "acceptance," "listening" does not make demands of the hearer beyond hearing, beyond a passive acknowledgement that something is occurring, that someone is present, that someone new is now at the table. But what about setting the table, determining the menu, deciding who gets to cook, who has to clean up, who is welcome to dine?

Listening alone is insufficient to the task of recognizing the full humanity, and capacity for self-determination, of those whose stories we hear. Merely hearing someone's story does not necessarily promote action. What, then, are the barriers to action on behalf of justice? This is where the work of feminist philosopher Miranda Fricker and theologian Erin Kidd pushed me beyond the paradigm of my first book, and toward the question of credibility. I realized, through their work, that listening means very little if we do not believe the story we are being told, and believability, credibility, is a privilege that is not equally distributed in our broken world. The fact is, women have been telling their stories of vocation, of abuse, of exclusion and marginalization in the Roman Catholic Church. They have also told their stories of the Holy Spirit at work in their lives, of their understanding of God embedded in their human experience, and of their hopes for a church that recognizes their full baptismal dignity. Women have been telling these stories for decades, if not centuries. But they remain at the margins of the institutional church, and these stories have often fallen on deaf ears.

In the penultimate chapter of John's Gospel, the evangelist directly addresses the reader (modern readers might call this "breaking the fourth wall" of the text), noting that Jesus did many other signs and wonders that are not written down in this particular book, but what is in the Gospel was "written so that you may come to believe...and that through believing you may have life in his name" (John 20:31). The next step in my feminist theological journey is to move from mere listening to something more powerful, more demanding, and infinitely more difficult. It is to move from hearing, even from listening and from dialogue to belief.

This lecture is an initial step in understanding why some people are more believable than others, and why women, especially women of color, simply aren't granted the credibility that persons, especially Euro-American men, have by virtue of their existence. I hope that in examining the intricacies of the credibility economy in which we are all embedded, the church may leave behind the shackles of epistemic injustice, and flourish into a discipleship of equals.

# Introduction

THANK YOU SO MUCH to Dr. Julia Feder, Dan Horan, and everyone at the St. Mary's Center for Spirituality, and thank you all for being here, and those who are watching too—especially the Feminist Theology students from Manhattan University. It's heartwarming to be back in South Bend among so many friends, colleagues, and former professors including my dissertation director Dr. Mary Catherine Hilkert. I have to confess that it is a lifelong dream realized to stand here ready to give this year's Madeleva lecture. Thirty-one years ago, in 1993, when I was a junior in high school, I read my first bit of feminist theology. It was a Madeleva lecture: Sandra Schneiders's *Women and the Word: The Gender of God in the New Testament and the Spirituality of Women* from 1986. Found on a shelf in the campus minister's office, I was drawn to the tiny book, thinking it would be an easy read if classes got boring. Boy, was I wrong. Schneider's words were nothing short of a revelation. The first four pages alone tackled God-language, gender, and women's ordination. Like any epiphany, reading that lecture was a moment of radiance. It reoriented my life, sparking ideas the fruition of which I would see only decades later. The notion that our understanding of God is conditioned by our language, and that in examining and changing our language we could come to grasp that God was beyond all our human understanding, even of gender, was a lot for a sixteen-year-old to grasp. But it was nothing short of lifechanging, and set me on a path that led me here, to the 2024 Madeleva Lecture. My overwhelming emotion right now is gratitude. My second feeling is the responsibility to shoulder the legacy of women who came before me in this role, and the obligation to do justice to their lives and their work.

The frame for this lecture rests on three experiences that constitute the origins of my thoughts on credibility, experience, and theology. While I have written on the importance of narrative as a methodological building block for contemporary ecclesiology, including in my book *Cuéntame*, the more I reflect (and live) the more I realize that the telling of stories is not enough. And so here are three moments that ground my interest in women's stories and credibility as a category, and three questions that will guide the remainder of this talk.

# I

# Experiential Foundations

THE FIRST EXPERIENCE begins in my first feminist theology class, at Fordham College Rose Hill. It was the fall semester of 1995, with Dr. Elizabeth Johnson, who laid out very systematically and very thoroughly the work that women had done in theology. We read the Bible against the grain with Phyllis Trible, Sandra Schneiders, and others, asked questions about the sexism inherent in Catholic theology with Mary Daly, Rosemary Radford Ruether, and others, and reconstructed the Christian message about God, about the church, about Christ with Johnson's own work. What an eye-opening semester! I moved through a cycle only possible for a sophomore in college: I loved it, giddily. I accepted it, enthusiastically. I embraced this new way of doing theology, moved on with it firmly in my theological toolbox. I naively thought "this is great, I'm so glad we've discovered this. We can do theology this way from now on." But by the time I was in a doctoral program, in a far more clergy-heavy setting, I realized that women's voices, women's thought and wisdom as part and parcel of any theological endeavor, wasn't a given in the majority of my courses. Too often, women's lives were studied as represented and theorized by men, and women scholars, along with scholars of color and other so-called contextual thought, were relegated to the last two weeks of the semester, when, I suppose, the "real" theology had been sufficiently covered and students had moved to reading less and focusing on their final papers more. Time and again it seemed there simply wasn't time to prioritize women's thoughts on Christology or ecclesiology or biblical studies. There weren't enough weeks in the semester to explore theology that wasn't done by men.

Of course, as I grew into this profession, I realized that course material, like citation practices, are a matter of priorities, of decisions. At times these decisions feel compulsory: how can we study X without covering the work of Foundational Thinker Y? But the longer we theologians, and professors in all disciplines, hide behind these canonical compulsions, the more obscure feminist thinking in theology becomes, the more we have to work to get our students, our parishes, our communities to understand that feminism, theology, and Catholicism can coexist and have, for decades.

Fast-forward nearly thirty years from 1995 to this semester. I find that when I am teaching feminist theology, or speaking about it, it continues to be breaking news to so many Catholics. Sr. Madeleva established her school in sacred theology in 1943, before my parents were born. Catholic women have been earning doctorates in theology for more than fifty years, and women have been thinking about God since there were women. And yet here I am, continually feeling like Sisyphus, rolling the same boulder up the same hill every semester, at every lecture. Audiences are astonished to hear that women interpret scripture, write theology, reflect on God's activity in their lives.

Why? One theory claims that this erasure is intentional. Toni Morrison famously claimed in a speech at Portland State University[1] that racism is a distraction keeping Black Americans busy justifying their existence instead of moving the antiracist cause forward. The same could be said of sexism. In this view, the patriarchy, the social order that is geared to the advantage of heterosexual white men, deliberately obscures women's thought, in this case their theological thought, so that each subsequent generation of thinkers has to retread the same ground. The goal is to make women waste their time, get frustrated, and give up, or at the very least, to slow the progress of breaking new ground, because we are constantly having to rebreak the same ground, justifying our existence as theological thinkers.

It is, indeed, a compelling theory that explains the near-constant erasure of women's voices in the academy. Is the Sisyphean task of introducing feminist theology again and again the result of a deliberate conspiracy on the part of the patriarchy? I think ultimately this theory attributes a level of deviousness and practical ability to carry out devious plans that I simply don't associate with most people. But then, why don't students know about feminist theology? Why don't church groups know? The hunger is there, the epiphanies still happen, but we are way past the point where these insights should be epiphanies. We should be two to three generations into women's theological production being common knowledge in Catholic circles. But it's not. I am reminded of the awful quote of Samuel Johnson two centuries ago: "A woman's preaching is like a dog's walking on his hind legs. It is not done well; but you are surprised to find it done at all."[2] How many people actually still think that?

Thus the first experience, which we will call the Sisyphus experience, prompts this question: Is there something about women doing theology that is inherently incredible or unbelievable?

Now on to experience number two: the testimony of Christine Blasey Ford in the Supreme Court confirmation hearings for Brett Kavanaugh. In my years of teaching, students are frequently horrified to learn about the common idea in ancient religious traditions that women couldn't testify in court because their word was worthless. They needed a man to prove they were telling the truth; they were treated like children, not like reliable witnesses. It seems preposterous and anachronistic until you watch Ford's testimony, which was perfect, and contained no inconsistencies. We watched a beautiful, white, well-educated woman telling what happened to her in as much detail and with as much recall as she could. It was convincing. It was moving. It reminded many of us of events in our own lives. And yet in the end, all the bravery and consistency and recall came to nothing. She had to leave her home amid death threats; he got a lifetime appointment to the highest court in the land. Her gut-wrenching testimony amounted to an idle tale, signifying nothing.

Collectively, publicly, women were reminded that it didn't matter how much or how clearly they remembered, it didn't matter how brave they were in coming forward or how perfect they were as victims or witnesses. Might made right, yet again. The failure of Blasey Ford's testimony was a huge blow, and another eye-opening experience, which prompted me to ask the following question: Today, in 2024, are women reliable narrators of their own experiences? Or has the justice system remained fundamentally unchanged? Why are we encouraged to "believe women" in slogans that prove controversial in the public sphere?

The third and final experience animating this lecture happened after my husband and I moved to New York. I was finishing my doctorate (it was my fifth year), and I was invited to be on a radio show with a priest for a Catholic radio network. Part of the process was to do a couple of audition tapings in a studio with the prospective cohost. At the time, I had just recently completed my comprehensive exams, so I was considered to be at the "all but dissertation" (ABD) stage, and I was very much in the throes of writing a dissertation on ecclesiology. The format of the radio show included call-in questions. And sometimes, during the answering part, I would answer because, well, I knew the answer. "Why does the church believe x?" And then I'd say, "This doctrine developed because of a, b, c in this context."

After a couple of these auditions in Manhattan, the executive in charge of communications for the diocese pulled me aside to "give me some notes." The note was this: listeners didn't want to hear me explaining church doctrine, they wanted to hear that from Father. "But... but...," I thought naively. "I'm the one who's about to get this PhD! I have ten years of theological study under my belt! He's got like, three to five years!" But it didn't matter, did it? Because the nameless faceless "listeners," and let's face it, the people in charge at the archdiocese didn't want to hear a woman in her twenties on the cusp of a doctoral degree in theology talking about doctrine when there was a priest right there. This brings us to my final question: Why is Father believable as a source of doctrinal knowledge or explanatory narrative but not Doctor or Professor or even an ABD graduate student with a lot of theological training?

These three experiences coalesce around the notion of credibility. How do we decide who we believe? And is it an individual, conscious decision, or are there structural factors at work in making some people more credible than others? Philosophers like Miranda Fricker, José Medina, and others argue that we are part of a "credibility economy"—a web of reciprocal relationships wherein there's an imbalance of power related to believability.[3] A person's believability varies depending on their social role but also depending on personal characteristics—marginalized persons generally suffer from a credibility deficit and persons from dominant social, economic, racial, and ethnic groups tend to enjoy a credibility excess in this economy.

# II

# Women's Experience in the Shadow of Epistemic Injustice

FOR A FAIR AMOUNT of the content of this lecture, I am indebted to the work of theologian Erin Kidd of St. John's University, particularly her engagement with Fricker's thought.[1] Dr. Fricker is a feminist philosopher who coined the term *epistemic injustice*. Epistemic injustice is a dense philosophical term made up of many parts, so let me attempt to unpack those here. Overall, Fricker (and Kidd) utilize epistemic injustice to highlight the intellectual imbalance associated with knowledge production and believability. So let's delve into it.

First, there are two kinds of epistemic injustice: distributive and discriminatory.[2] Distributive epistemic injustice refers to the distribution of, or access to, goods pertaining to knowledge: education, information, internet access, books. We do not all have equal access to education and the rest of these things, therefore, injustice is present. If you are poor, or from a marginalized community, you have a harder time gaining access to education. So on one level, we don't all equally know because we don't all have equal access to how we get knowledge.

The second kind of epistemic injustice is discriminatory: if distributive injustice is about access to knowledge goods, then discriminatory injustice is more about increasing/decreasing credibility, or based on prejudice. That prejudice can be individual or structural. This is where epistemic injustice intersects with feminist theology in important ways, for me. Individual discriminatory epistemic injustice (a mouthful) I will also just call "testimonial" injustice, where the structural variety might be termed hermeneutic injustice. While these are not exact parallels, they are a practical way of thinking about this complex reality.

What makes a person credible? Credibility attaches to a person either because of their role or because of personal characteristics. Similarly, these can cause credibility to decrease. Individually, a hearer can be prejudiced: Maria says something but there is a quality about her that I find inherently distasteful or untrustworthy, which causes me not to put my trust in her word. I give her less credibility. So, for instance, if I am prejudiced against nonwhite persons, then I am not inclined to believe them, I perceive them as less credible. If I believed, for example, that redhaired people are inherently untrustworthy and therefore more likely to lie, then if a redhead reports a crime, I am suspicious. I don't trust that person's word. That is testimonial injustice.

Women suffer from testimonial injustice regularly—and have historically, as we saw in the case of Dr. Ford, and of many survivors of sexual violence before and since. Our society's stereotypes about women as flighty or emotional have rendered women's word less trustworthy, and women less believable, because we associate emotions with volatility and accuracy with unwavering, cold intellectual rigor. Dr. Kidd points out in her work that we also see testimonial injustice in the case of clerical sex abuse survivors, but in a bit of a different key, since many of those survivors who came forward initially were men. That testimonial injustice did not happen because of prejudice against the person testifying (initially mostly men, many of whom were white). Instead, the injustice stemmed from a level of role-incredulity. Objections claiming that the abuse simply could not have happened, because the victim was talking about a priest, and there was no way a priest could do those terrible things all stem from testimonial injustice.[3]

Testimonial injustice, then, can go both ways: a credibility deficit (someone we don't trust because of who they are) or a credibility excess, someone we are inclined to believe because of who they are. For years and years, clergy enjoyed an excess of credibility because Catholics associated the priesthood with a special kind of holiness, connected both to the theology of the "ontological change" that takes place at ordination but also because of cultural structures that offered ordained men special status and privileges, including "closeness to God." The clerical state of life was believed to be higher than the lay state, and therefore clergy were higher up on the holiness ladder. Perhaps this is why radio listeners don't want to hear a layperson talk about church doctrine, because the clergy has, or had, a credibility excess.

A second example of this credibility variance can be seen in student course evaluations. We are taught to expect "experts" to look a certain way and when they don't, we struggle to make sense of it. This conflict between appearances and reality leads to a slew of problems inherent in student evaluations of college courses. A study published in 2016 shows that American students reliably rate white, male, heterosexual professors with no accents higher across the board in course evaluations than professors who deviate from these characteristics. Male professors are twice or three times more likely to be described as "brilliant" or "genius" by their students, whereas women are more likely to be described according to affective terms like "nice" or "not nice."[4] Women who conform to gender roles (like nurturing, kindness, gentleness) score higher, but still overall lower, than men who do, given that their prescribed gender role includes intelligence. Women professors, and this is exacerbated intersectionally with the compounding prejudices of race, gender, sexual orientation, and language proficiency, simply cannot attain the level of brilliance of their male counterparts, because students (and truly, all of us) are trained not to believe that experts look like women. Again, this credibility deficit coincides with the phenomenon of role incredulity—experts aren't supposed to look like Black women, so students tend to disbelieve Black women professors.

Women, as a group, have long suffered a credibility deficit, and this is exacerbated by other bits of marginalization: race, gender identity, sexual orientation, wealth. We've seen how intersectional analysis, and the identities revealed therewith, locate problems with credibility in our country's long history with racism, for example. Intersectional analysis of the credibility economy leads to some surprising inversions. The case of Emmett Till is only one instance where a white woman's credibility deficit (for being a woman) was nevertheless enough to override the credibility deficit of a young Black man. He paid with his life for that particular instance of testimonial injustice.

Testimonial injustice harms us all: it predisposes us to disbelieve people who are historically disempowered or marginalized, and it enables us to believe the powerful because we associate them with virtue in some way.

But credibility deficits don't just happen on an individual level. If it were only an individual problem, then we could simply root out the prejudiced individuals and the problem would be fixed. But like all our prejudices, there is a structural component to epistemic injustice. Dr. Fricker calls this structural component "hermeneutical injustice," a type of injustice that has to do with interpretation. Think of it as "shut out of the storytelling" injustice. Hermeneutical injustice happens when a marginalized group is excluded from the social process of meaning-making and therefore lacks the words, the concepts, the interpretive tools to explain their experiences to others or even to understand these experiences themselves. Fricker terms this a gap in collective understanding that exists because of the relative powerlessness or isolation of the people experiencing that situation.[5] This gap can be best illustrated using examples.

Let us consider the case of the phrases *domestic violence* and/or *marital rape*. Until our very recent past, it was inconceivable that either of these behaviors would constitute a crime. The legal system consisted of men, who were charged with making and interpreting laws. In this system, women were not viewed as full human beings, but possessions or children. The criminalization of domestic violence took a long time, and it was helped along very much by the invention of the Polaroid camera, which allowed women to retain evidence of bruises and other signs of violence as backup to their word.[6] Intimate partner violence, as we now refer to domestic violence remains ubiquitous, but underreported. Advocacy organizations estimate 35 percent of women and 25 percent of men experience some kind of intimate partner violence in their lifetime. The number is higher for college students. As we know, the prevalence of sexual assault on college campuses is staggering, and the dearth of prosecutions for these crimes is equally astonishing. Only since the advent of consciousness-raising groups in second-wave feminism and subsequently have women been able to come together and recognize those "yeah, yeah" moments that made their marriages, their work lives, or their college experiences unbearable.

More frighteningly, women's exclusion from social

meaning-making affected our understanding of the institution of marriage. Historically and even sacramentally to some extent, marriage was understood as a contract providing a safe haven for male lust, or as a place where men could satisfy sexual urges. This meant that the concept of rape or unwanted sexual contact within a marriage was inconceivable—it was the woman's obligation to have sex with her husband. This was even colloquially known as the marital debt. If sexual relations are framed as a debt, then refusing to pay is the crime, not collecting the debt. Marital rape was very rarely considered possible before the 1970s, and was not criminalized in all fifty states until 1993—the very year I read Schneiders's Madeleva lecture. It's a hermeneutical injustice because the way women were taught to talk about marriage included willingness to have sex; there wasn't room in the story for being coerced, or worse. Consent was not part of the discussion because it was assumed in the "I do" of the marriage story. That story, we know, was too narrow, because the story was constructed without women's input. Even women couldn't conceptualize marital rape, because the paradigm of marriage relegated them to objects for men's fulfillment.

A religious example of hermeneutical injustice, of the unimaginability of a ubiquitous experience, is available to us in the work of Judith Plaskow, the Jewish feminist theologian. Halakhic codes in scripture such as Deuteronomy 22:28 dictated that the punishment for a man raping a virgin was financial restitution to the woman's father and also his agreeing to marry her. Plaskow asks how it is possible that the punishment for rape be that a woman "gets" to marry her rapist.[7] And the answer, of course, is that this law was elaborated entirely from the perspective of men. Only a man would view that as a just punishment for the rapist and not a complete trauma for the victim. The only way that story is plausible is if women are considered property, not people. The story of what marriage was, what sex was, what women were, was too narrow. By excluding women from the community of meaning-making and sense-making, lawmakers ancient and modern blinded themselves to the reality of women's bodily integrity and dignity.

Given the wide-ranging nature and diverse components of epistemic injustice that we've outlined: distributive, discriminatory, testimonial, and hermeneutic, we must ask where the points of intersection and creative friction between this philosophical understanding and women's theological production might occur.

For Dr. Kidd, epistemic injustice is a key category in how we minister to survivors of sexual assault both in the church and outside of it. Consistent exposure to hermeneutical and testimonial injustice, says Kidd, does theological harm because it prevents a victim's spiritual formation and therefore her relationship with God. We should, therefore, retrain our testimonial sensibility and view survivor testimonies as dangerous memories that help reframe our thinking and our theological imaginations.

# III

# The Church and the Credibility Economy

MY INTERESTS MOVE beyond the individual harm to Catholics who suffer from a credibility deficit or who are subjected to testimonial injustice and toward the communal (ecclesial) harm done by this injustice. Dr. Kidd suggests that "who does theology and whose theology is listened to matters. So we should look at the demographics of who historically has done theology, who is ordained, and whose theology is read in seminaries, who can preach in Christian churches,"[1] to get a sense of where our epistemic injustice is rooted. Not only does epistemic injustice harm an individual in her quest for spiritual development, to be known understood herself as loved by God, but epistemic injustice also harms the church as a communal entity, and prevents it from being a sacrament of salvation by blinding the church to the complexities of human dignity, to the gifts of those without a credibility excess, to the authority of those who suffer role incredulity.

Judith Plaskow makes a radical claim in her *Standing again at Sinai*, arguing that since the Torah records the impressions and revelations of God's self to men, there cannot truly be Judaism without the Torah revealed to women, which women must create. Similarly, I'd like to argue that the Catholic Church is hopelessly handicapped, is less than what it needs to be, as long as it continues to ignore theology done by women, as long as women suffer from the epistemic injustice perpetrated by clericalism and by deficient dogmatic understandings of women's nature. As long as women are shut out of theological conversations, out of seminaries and out of ordained ministry, the church fails to witness to the fullness of the reality of God. How? I will outline three critical ways.

First, the gender story told by the church, complementarianism, exemplifies hermeneutical injustice. Claiming exemption from "gender theory," the Vatican has nevertheless time and again asserted that men and women are different but complementary. Complementarity is a theoretical system that is binary in nature and ultimately relies on an essentialist, "biology is destiny" kind of reasoning: women have uteruses therefore are meant to make space for the other. Men are, in teachings that are undergirded by an Aristotelian/Thomistic mashup for the ages, the "active principle in sex" therefore are the principal actors in public life, in decision making, and in their families. Women are nurturing and emotional, men are pragmatic and intellectual.

This binary notion of gender is increasingly outdated and unscientific, but the church continues to double down on it!

John Paul II asserted in *Mulieris Dignitatem* that women possess a universal vocation to maternity, whether physical or spiritual. Of course, we know that many women cannot be mothers, and many more will not be mothers, physically or spiritually, because that is simply not their life's path. But the binary, reified gender story is so powerful that despite the many persons who proclaim themselves exceptions to this gender story, and the many ways that the church acknowledges the inadequacy of John Paul II's stance on women and motherhood (such as acknowledging that infertility is not a sin but just another physical reality, or blessing the marriages of elderly people who cannot procreate), as a church we cannot seem to break out of it in theological language. And so we find even Pope Francis's Dicastery for the Doctrine of the Faith, despite its progressive stances on so many issues, rendered incapable of talking about women as anything but enhancements, albeit important enhancements, to the church's project. Francis famously called women theologians the strawberries on the theological cake. More recently he said that women bring beauty and care to the world—always softness, always aesthetics, always a gentleness that is a complement to men's harsh, unwavering, uncaring rationality. Excluding women from meaning-making results in an image of women always in-relation, never self-determined but rather determined by the male other as mother, as wife, as bride, as nurturer, as adornment, presumably to please a male God. Structurally enforced hermeneutical injustice prevents women from naming the revelation they have received, and when they do, it is classified as mysticism, or reflection, or beauty. The magisterium lacks a category for women's theological rigor because their gender theory excludes women epistemologically, as knowers. Women as anything but persons-in-relation becomes a category that, as José Medina notes, suffers from the sin of unimaginability—beyond ignorance, the incapacity to conceive of something.

Unimaginability exists, too, in our church's pervasive commitment to the maleness of God, nearly forty years after Sandra Schneiders stood here and even more since Mary Daly noted the correlation between God's imagined gender and the social hierarchy we see on earth. Ecclesially, this magisterium's continued commitment to the so-called Marian and Petrine principles in the church hobbles the people of God by shoehorning the church into a binary that is both nonbiblical and nonsensical. Despite women's protests, despite the ease with which these binary principles crumble when, for example, theologians are forced to make the case that laymen are part of the Marian principle but women cannot for any reason participate in the Petrine one, the Vatican remains steadfast in its dedication to this Balthasarian imagery. The binary proves to be quite fragile under scrutiny and yet it enjoys prominence in official church documents—might this be because of the credibility excess of thinkers like Hans Urs von Balthasar among the clerical class? All talk of "respecting" women and their vocations, of valuing women as decision makers and givers of input, remains a marginal possibility at best as long as these categories remain in vogue.

My last point is about women's credibility deficit, and the credibility deficit of all non-clergy in our hierarchical church. Much has been made in Francis's pontificate of becoming a "listening church." We can look to the ongoing synod as a prime example of an attempt at becoming such a church—a church that listens to those on the margins, a church that listens to the poor and disenfranchised. As promising as it all sounds, it cannot help but fall short. I confess here that I am doubtful that the synod's various sessions will come to any significant change. Time and again women have been forced to learn the harsh reality that listening is not enough. Notably, in July, when the members of the Synod's ten working groups were revealed, the names in the group tasked with investigating the possibility of women deacons were not made public.[2] While this does not indicate a decision on the matter of women deacons, the lack of transparency with this specific working group and no others does not inspire great hope.

# IV

# Conclusions

IN SOME OF MY previous work, I've noted that it is not sufficient to "add Latinos and stir" to our theologies in order for them to be inclusive. For theology to include the voices of marginalized racial and ethnic communities, these communities must be allowed to drive and set priorities, to be presented in the beginnings of courses, not at the end as some enhancement. I'm afraid that the concept of "listening" church suffers from this "and stir" optimism that is ultimately insufficient. Because as a church we must go beyond listening to women, we have to believe them. Believe them to be narrators of their experience, believe them to be dialogue partners with God, believe them to be capable theologians and scripture scholars and interpreters of God's activity in their lives and in the wider world. Listening alone is not enough. We all listened to Christine Blasey Ford. We listened to Anita Hill. We listen when we are presented with a theological perspective from Hildegard of Bingen or Teresa of Ávila. You're listening to me right now! But do you believe me? Are we not, as feminist theologians, consistently reminded that persons in our role simply do not look like we do, that role incredulity is part and parcel of this vocation?

And yet, there are seeds in the Gospel that point toward a remedy for the widespread epistemic, testimonial, hermeneutic injustice women suffer in our church's credibility economy. I want to finish with a foundational Gospel story that speaks to me about credibility deficits and how the church has used this concept, even without naming it as such, from its very beginnings. It's from Luke's account of the resurrection, and also the tip-off for the title of this talk. Women appearing as key figures among the earliest Christians is widely recognized as a scandalous admission, and women appearing by name in the Gospels is very rare indeed. But in all four evangelists' accounts, Mary Magdalene is among the first to see the risen Christ. Luke phrases it like this:

> And returning from the tomb, they told all this to the eleven and to all the rest. Now it was Mary Magdalene, Joanna, Mary the mother of James, and the other women with them who told this to the apostles. But these words seemed to them an idle tale, and they [the eleven] did not believe them. But Peter got up and ran to the tomb; stooping and looking in, he saw the linen cloths by themselves; then he went home, amazed at what had happened. (Luke 24:9–12)

The eleven *listened* to Mary Magdalene, but they did not *believe* her. Peter didn't really believe her, he had to go see for himself. But the Gospel writers include Mary Magdalene's testimony in the stories of the resurrection, even though it was embarrassing to them to have the central claim of Christianity rely on the previously worthless testimony of a woman, as New Testament scholar Claudia Setzer has noted.[1] After all, the earliest Christians were fighting claims of being too egalitarian and effeminate in their religiosity, so having a woman be the testimonial lynchpin to the resurrection is scandalous. But as I learned from my feminist theologian professors, and my Madaleva predecessors, this "embarrassment criterion" is a testament to the truth of Magdalene's witness, that the community is willing to risk embarrassment, shame and scandal to tell the truth about the resurrection. It would have been easier to leave it out.

The eleven men caricature Mary Magdalene and the other women as bearers of an idle tale. They suffered from a credibility deficit, and also from a hermeneutical impossibility—the unimaginability of a thing like resurrection—people didn't rise from the dead. So they listened, but they did not believe.

On the other hand, the church we inherit from the apostles *does* believe Mary Magdalene's testimony. The church exists as a witness to our belief in her story. The resurrection accounts in the Gospels invite us to believe, in fact, they demand that we believe the testimony of the Magdalene. Can we get back there again? Can we look at Mary Magdalene and see neither a prostitute or a teller of idle tales, but instead see a woman who bears the good news? An apostle to the apostles? And if we can see apostolicity, preaching, prophetic ecclesial awareness in Mary Magdalene, what will it take so we can see it, hear it, *believe* it in women today?

Attempting to find an answer to the credibility problem is as complex as the problem itself. Different aspects that give rise to a credibility deficit require different approaches. Let us take, for example, the notion of role incredulity. One reason Catholics assume their priest knows what he is talking about when it comes to scripture, faith, and theology is because the priest is who they see on Sundays preaching a homily, ideally about the scriptures for that week and the application of those readings to the contemporary life of faith. The assumption is that the priest has many years of training, practice, and experience in living the scriptures. Indeed, it is this excess of credibility, when it bleeds into "therefore the priest is necessarily a holy and good man, incapable of horrific sin," that makes abusive cultures so pervasive.

How to move beyond this? A crucial first step is to invite lay preaching into Sunday worship. The gift of preaching is a charism, and as such, we can expect that the Holy Spirit does not confine this gift to those who have received holy orders. It may be that members of our parishes who are not ordained do in fact have a gift for preaching. This is not to say that we should pick parishioners at random. But groups such as Catholic Women Preach, FutureChurch, and others have successfully built platforms where Catholics can hear women who are scholars or longtime ministers reflect upon the scriptures and their application to our contemporary lives of faith. These platforms, most of which feature text and videos, allow us to see women doing the work of preaching. How much more powerful would it be to have a woman step up to the pulpit after the Gospel is read to offer a reflection or even, if we dare call it so, a homily?

Inviting women to preach at Mass would also expose more Catholics to the reality of preaching-as-charism and the reality that many women have the training and the gift of opening up the scriptures through uncommonly used lenses and contexts. Making this a regular part of a Catholic's churchgoing experience would lend a "normalcy" to the idea that women are capable of theological knowledge. The experience would, one hopes, open up the possibility of seeing women as experts in God-talk, scriptural interpretation, inspiration of the faithful. These things build credibility; they scaffold the possibility of not only hearing women on a particular Sunday but of believing women to be capable theologians on the other days of the week.

There is an additional benefit to having women preach from the pulpit in a liturgical context, instead of doing it exclusively in video or text formats. Having women share liturgical space with men reminds the people of God that all of us, clergy and lay, approach the altar with similar status as sinners who seek redemption in and through the paschal mystery.

Think of the experience of a child watching a priest

or deacon preach. There is no recognition in that child's universe that the person preaching is "ontologically different," nor any conception that there is a sacrament that sets that person apart from the mothers and sisters all around her. What that child likely assumes instead, from an early age, that the person in the pulpit has special authority to tell the truth, to reveal God's word, specifically because of the place that person holds in the congregation. The child both *listens* and *believes*, but the factors that bring him or her to that point have nothing to do with theology; they are social constructs, like the various kinds of discrimination and cultural assumptions I have discussed at length above.

What might a child who listened to a woman on a regular basis do such preaching learn, or assume? No longer would the story of Mary Magdalene be an anomaly, but a constituent experience of all in the church. Unlike the apostles in the aforementioned Gospel story, unlike generations and generations of Catholics culturally conditioned to equate Christian belief with the structures and assumptions of Christendom, that child might instead recognize a fellow disciple breaking open the word—and thus *hear*, *listen*, and *believe*.

# Notes

## I.
## EXPERIENTIAL FOUNDATIONS

1. Toni Morrison, "A Humanist View," from Portland State University's Oregon Public Speakers Collection: "Black Studies Center Public Dialogue. Pt. 2," May 30, 1975 (http://bit.ly/1vO2hLP). Part of the Public Dialogue on the American Dream Theme, via Portland State University Library (http://bit.ly/1q8HG3h).

2. Thomas Boswell, *The Life of Samuel Johnson*, ed. and notes by Roger Ingpen (London: Sir Isaac Pitman and Sons, 1907), 280.

3. Miranda Fricker, *Epistemic Injustice: Power & the Ethics of Knowing* (New York: Oxford University Press, 2007); José Medina, *Epistemologies of Resistance: Gender and Racial Oppression, Epistemic Injustice, and Resistant Imaginations* (New York: Oxford, 2013).

## II.
## WOMEN'S EXPERIENCE IN THE SHADOW OF EPISTEMIC INJUSTICE

1. Erin Kidd, "Feminist Theology of Testimony," *Theological Studies*, 83, no. 3 (2022): 424–42.

2. My understanding of Dr. Fricker's work in this section especially is indebted to Dr. Kidd's article and also to Kelly Louise Rexzy P. Agra, "Epistemic Injustice, Epistemic Paralysis, and Epistemic Resistance: A (Feminist) Liberatory Approach to Epistemology," *Kritike* 14, no. 1 (June 2020): 28–44. Both scholars' exposition of Fricker's work is invaluable.

3. See Erin Kidd, "Theology in the Wake of Survivor Testimony: Epistemic Injustice and Clergy Sex Abuse," *Journal of Religion & Society*, Supplement 21 (2020): 171–72, http://hdl.handle.net/10504/126219.

4. Daniel Storage, Zachary Horne, Andrei Cimpian, and Sarah-Jane Leslie, "The Frequency of 'Brilliant' and 'Genius' in Teaching Evaluations Predicts the Representation of Women and African Americans across Fields," PLoS ONE 11, no. 3 (2016): e0150194. https://doi:10.1371/journal. pone.0150194.

5. Susan Dieleman, "An Interview with Miranda Fricker," *Social Epistemology* 26, no. 2 (2012): 256.

6. Esta Soler, "How We Turned the Tide on Domestic Violence," TEDWomen talk available at: https://www.ted.com/talks/esta_soler_how_we_turned_the_tide_on_domestic_violence_hint_the_polaroid_helped/transcript?subtitle=en. Soler is the founder of Futures

without Violence. She delivered this TEDWomen talk in 2013.

7. Judith Plaskow, *Standing again at Sinai: Judaism from a Feminist Perspective* (New York: HarperCollins, 1991), 4, 172–75.

## III.
## THE CHURCH AND THE CREDIBILITY ECONOMY

1. Kidd, *Survivor Testimony*, 14.

2. See Chris White's reporting in NCR: https://www.ncronline.org/vatican/vatican-news/vatican-synod-agenda-calls-transparency-women-deacons-its-lacking.

## IV.
## CONCLUSIONS

1. Claudia Setzer, "Excellent Women: Female Witness to the Resurrection," *Journal of Biblical Literature* 116, no. 2 (1997): 259–72.

# WOMEN, EARTH, AND CREATOR SPIRIT

Revised Edition

*Elizabeth A. Johnson*

Makes the point that the social domination of women and the ecological domination of the earth are inextricably fused in theory and practice.

5637-5 • $14.95

# WOMEN AND PUBLIC THEOLOGY

## Emerging Voices

*Edited by Elissa Cutter and Allison Murray*

Even in the twenty-first century, women working in the field of Christian theology still find it necessary to insist on being heard. In order to provide a platform for these women, the blog *Women in Theology* (*WIT*) was started, which hosts contributions from a spectrum of Christian traditions, Catholic, Eastern Orthodox, and Protestant.

This collection is a curated and edited selection of posts from *WIT* along with new pieces from regular *WIT* contributors.

5610-8 • $29.95

## DIVINE INTERRUPTIONS

Maternal Theologies and Experiences

*Edited by Cristina Lledo Gomez and Julia H. Brumbaugh*

This book promotes feminist-maternal theological reflections as vital sources and lenses from and through which to consider both classical and contemporary topics of the systematic theological corpus. Feminist-maternal theologies particularly resist Church Christian theologian traditions that are tempted time and again to reduce the idea of mothering into simplistic, static, infantile, and largely biologically based pictures of mothers and women, and their relationships to children.

5599-6 • $49.95

# HEART, TEARS, FRUITS

## The Search for a Feminine Theology

*edited by Lucinda M. Vardey*

This book stems from a series of seminars in response to Pope Francis's call for a profound feminine theology.

5685-6 • $14.95

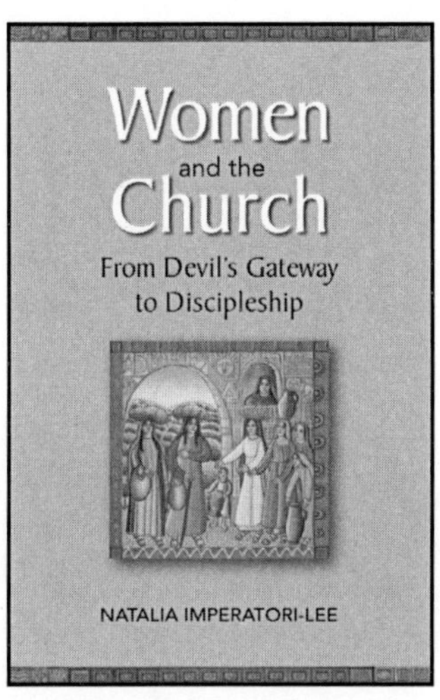
Women
and the
Church
From Devil's Gateway
to Discipleship
NATALIA IMPERATORI-LEE